United States Government Accountability Office

Report to the Committee on Oversight and Government Reform, House of Representatives

I0448564

September 2013

FREEDOM OF INFORMATION ACT

Office of Government Information Services Has Begun Implementing Its Responsibilities, but Further Actions Are Needed

GAO-13-650

FREEDOM OF INFORMATION ACT

Office of Government Information Services Has Begun Implementing Its Responsibilities, but Further Actions Are Needed

GAO Highlights

Highlights of GAO-13-650, a report to the Committee on Oversight and Government Reform, House of Representatives

Why GAO Did This Study

The *OPEN Government Act of 2007* amended FOIA and established OGIS within the National Archives and Records Administration to provide oversight and assistance to federal agencies in implementing FOIA. To evaluate how effectively the office is meeting its responsibilities, GAO assessed the actions that the office has taken to (1) implement its responsibilities for reviewing agencies' policies, procedures, and compliance with FOIA; (2) mediate disputes between FOIA requesters and federal agencies; and (3) recommend policy changes to Congress and the President and develop and issue guidance and best practices to improve the administration of FOIA. To do so, GAO analyzed documents describing the office's plans and activities for conducting reviews, mediation case files, and documents describing its policy recommendations made to Congress and the President and its guidance and best practices. GAO also interviewed officials at relevant agencies.

What GAO Recommends

GAO is recommending that OGIS fulfill its statutory responsibilities by establishing (1) a time frame for completing and implementing a methodology for proactively reviewing agencies' policies, procedures, and compliance with FOIA requirements and (2) measures and goals for its mediation services. In written comments on a draft of the report, the National Archives and Records Administration concurred with the recommendations.

View GAO-13-650. For more information, contact Valerie C. Melvin at (202) 512-6304 or melvinv@gao.gov.

What GAO Found

Since its establishment in 2009, the Office of Government Information Services (OGIS) has provided comments on proposed *Freedom of Information Act* (FOIA) regulations for 18 of 99 federal agencies that administer FOIA, as well as a number of *Privacy Act* system of records notices. While OGIS has suggested improvements to a number of those regulations and notices, it has not performed the reviews of regulations and notices in a proactive, comprehensive manner, and has not conducted any reviews of agencies' compliance with the law. In addition, since it was established 4 years ago, the office has not developed a methodology for conducting reviews of agencies' FOIA policies and procedures, or for compliance with FOIA requirements. OGIS is in the early stages of developing a methodology for conducting such reviews, but has not established a time frame for completion. Until OGIS establishes a methodology and time frame for proactively reviewing agencies' FOIA policies, procedures, and compliance, the office will not be positioned to effectively execute its responsibilities as required by the act.

OGIS is providing mediation services and is resolving disputes that might otherwise go unresolved or lead to litigation, although not all of its efforts have been successful. OGIS has achieved positive results for about two-thirds of the cases reviewed by GAO where mediation services were provided. For example, in several cases, one or both parties took action or modified their position after OGIS's intervention. Nevertheless, the office lacks quantifiable goals and measures for its mediation activities, as required by law. For example, it does not have goals to measure timeliness or success. Without these important management tools, OGIS cannot determine how effectively its mediation services are in improving the implementation of FOIA.

Since April 2012, OGIS has issued nine recommendations to Congress and the President aimed at improving the administration of FOIA. These recommendations focus on areas where OGIS could help agencies improve their FOIA processes as well as areas where its role could be made more effective. These recommendations were based on its ongoing work with federal agencies and with members of the public. In addition, while not required to issue guidance or best practices, the office collects best practices for improving FOIA processing from several sources, including its reviews of agencies' annual FOIA reports and mediation case files, as well as anecdotally from persons involved in mediation cases facilitated by the office. OGIS shares these best practices in its annual reports and on its website and blog.

Contents

GAO U.S. GOVERNMENT ACCOUNTABILITY OFFICE

441 G St. N.W.
Washington, DC 20548

September 10, 2013

The Honorable Darrell E. Issa
Chairman
The Honorable Elijah E. Cummings
Ranking Member
Committee on Oversight and Government Reform
House of Representatives

The *Freedom of Information Act* (FOIA)[1] requires federal agencies to provide the public with access to government records and information on the basis of the principles of openness and accountability in government. In this regard, each year hundreds of thousands of FOIA requests are made to federal agencies—with the information released in response to these requests contributing to the disclosure of government waste, fraud, and abuse, as well as other conditions, such as unsafe consumer products and harmful drugs. However, keeping up with this demand for information and responding in a timely manner has been challenging for federal agencies. Congress, in turn, has amended the act to guide agencies in the administration of their FOIA operations. One such enactment—the *OPEN Government Act of 2007*[2]—established the Office of Government Information Services (OGIS) within the National Archives and Records Administration (NARA) to oversee and assist agencies in implementing FOIA. Toward this end, the office was charged with reviewing federal agencies' FOIA policies and procedures and their compliance with FOIA, and recommending policy changes to Congress and the President to improve the administration of FOIA. Additionally, OGIS was required to offer mediation services to resolve disputes between FOIA requesters and agencies.

Given the important role that OGIS has been assigned, we were requested to evaluate how effectively the office is meeting its responsibilities. In particular, our objectives were to assess the actions that the office has taken to (1) review agencies' FOIA policies, procedures, and compliance; (2) mediate disputes between FOIA

---

[1] 5 U.S.C. § 552.

[2] The *Openness Promotes Effectiveness in our National (OPEN) Government Act of 2007*, Pub. L. No. 110-175 (Dec. 31, 2007).

requesters and federal agencies; and (3) recommend policy changes to Congress and the President, and develop and issue guidance and best practices to agencies aimed at improving the administration of FOIA.

To assess the actions that OGIS has taken to review federal agencies' FOIA policies, procedures, and compliance, we analyzed available documentation describing the office's plans and activities for conducting agency reviews. This included OGIS's annual reports and quarterly progress reports that summarized its plans and activities. We also analyzed the office's comments on proposed agency regulations, *Privacy Act of 1974*[3] system of records notices,[4] and correspondence. In analyzing OGIS's plans for conducting agency reviews, we applied program evaluation guidance[5] that focuses on assessing the effectiveness of program operations and results.

To assess OGIS's actions in mediating disputes between FOIA requesters and federal agencies, we reviewed, among other things, laws addressing federal mediation activities, published literature on mediation, and the office's documented procedures for mediating disputes. Using OGIS's case tracking system, we selected and reviewed the 44 cases[6] that were initiated in fiscal year 2012 and were characterized by the office as involving facilitation, a type of mediation. We also reviewed the corresponding paper files documenting the actions taken and the results of mediation activities for these cases. To determine the reliability of the data in the system, we performed steps to ensure the data provided were valid and reviewed how data are entered and validated. We tested duplicate records, missing values, and out-of-range values. We found the data sources to be sufficiently reliable for our purposes.

---

[3]5 U.S.C. § 552a.

[4]*The Privacy Act of 1974* requires agencies to publish system of records notices in the Federal Register to descr be holdings of personal information in covered system of records. 5 U.S.C. § 552a(e)(4).

[5]GAO, *Designing Evaluations: 2012 Revision*, GAO-12-208G (Washington, D.C.: January 2012).

[6]While 46 cases were initiated in 2012, we included 44 cases in our review. One case was omitted because it involved only OGIS and agency officials, and a second was omitted because the case was not included in the data OGIS provided from which we made our selection.

To assess the office's actions to recommend policy changes to Congress and the President, we analyzed its documents describing policy recommendations that were made to Congress and the President. In addition, we reviewed the Office of Management and Budget's (OMB) written responses describing its reviews of OGIS's policy recommendations and any applicable OMB guidance, such as the Circular A-19[7] and we interviewed officials from OMB's Office of General Counsel. In addition, to assess OGIS's actions to develop and issue guidance and best practices to federal agencies, we analyzed documentation on OGIS's agency best practices, case studies, and the office's suggestions regarding FOIA implementation. We supplemented our analyses with interviews of NARA and OGIS officials.

We conducted this performance audit from October 2012 through September 2013 in accordance with generally accepted government auditing standards. Those standards require that we plan and perform the audit to obtain sufficient, appropriate evidence to provide a reasonable basis for our findings and conclusions based on our audit objectives. We believe that the evidence obtained provides a reasonable basis for our findings and conclusions based on our audit objectives. Appendix I contains a more detailed discussion of our objectives, scope, and methodology.

Background

FOIA established a legal right of access to government information on the basis of the principles of openness and accountability in government. Prior to passage of the act in 1966, the government required an individual or entity to demonstrate a "need to know" before being granted the right to examine a federal record. FOIA established a "right to know" standard, under which an individual or entity could receive access to information held by a federal agency without demonstrating a need or reason. The "right to know" standard shifted the burden of proof from the individual or entity to the government agency holding the information and required the agency to provide proper justification when denying a request for access.

Any person, with a few exceptions, can file a FOIA request, including foreign nationals, corporations, and organizations. For example, a foreign

---

[7]Office of Management and Budget, *Legislative Coordination and Clearance,* Circular No. A-19, (Washington, D.C.: Sept. 20, 1979).

national can request his or her alien file, and a commercial requester, which can include data brokers that file a request on behalf of others, may request, among other things, a copy of a government contract or grant proposal. In response, the agency holding the desired record is required to provide it to the requester (unless the record falls within a permitted exemption).[8] Generally, FOIA allows agencies to collect a fee for searching and duplicating records in connection with responding to a request. Apart from providing access to records in response to a request, FOIA also requires agencies to disclose certain information by publication in the *Federal Register* or electronically (e.g., on the Internet), or by making it available in a physical or electronic reading room.

While FOIA has helped improve public access to government information and has been a positive step toward providing more openness in government, a March 12, 2007, House committee report accompanying the *OPEN Government Act*[9] pointed out that agencies receive hundreds of thousands of FOIA requests a year, which has led to slow response times, increased backlogs, and costly and time-consuming litigation between requesters and the government. As such, according to the report, FOIA requesters have argued that they would benefit from having access to an ombudsman to provide guidance before, or as an alternative to, litigation.

OGIS Was Established to Help Oversee the Administration of FOIA

To help address the concerns surrounding FOIA implementation, the *OPEN Government Act*,[10] among other things, established OGIS within NARA to:

- review policies and procedures that agencies have developed to administer FOIA;
- review agency compliance with FOIA requirements;
- recommend policy changes to Congress and the President to improve the administration of FOIA; and

---

[8]Nine specific exemptions can be applied to withhold a requested record, for example, classified, confidential commercial, pre-decisional, privacy, and several types of law enforcement information.

[9]Committee on Oversight and Government Reform, *Freedom of Information Act Amendments of 2007*, House Rep. No. 110-45 (2007).

[10]Pub. L. No. 110-175 (Dec. 31, 2007).

- offer mediation services to resolve disputes between individuals or entities making FOIA requests and agencies as an non-exclusive alternative to litigation.

OGIS was established within NARA, on September 8, 2009. The office operated directly under the Archivist of the United States until March 7, 2011, when it was moved to Agency Services, which operates under the authority of the agency's Chief Operating Officer. According to its charter, the mission of Agency Services is to lead NARA's efforts in servicing the ongoing records management needs of federal agencies and to represent the public's interest in the accountability and transparency of these records. OGIS is one of five supporting offices under Agency Services, as shown on the organization chart in figure 1.

Figure 1: Organizational Chart Depicting OGIS within NARA

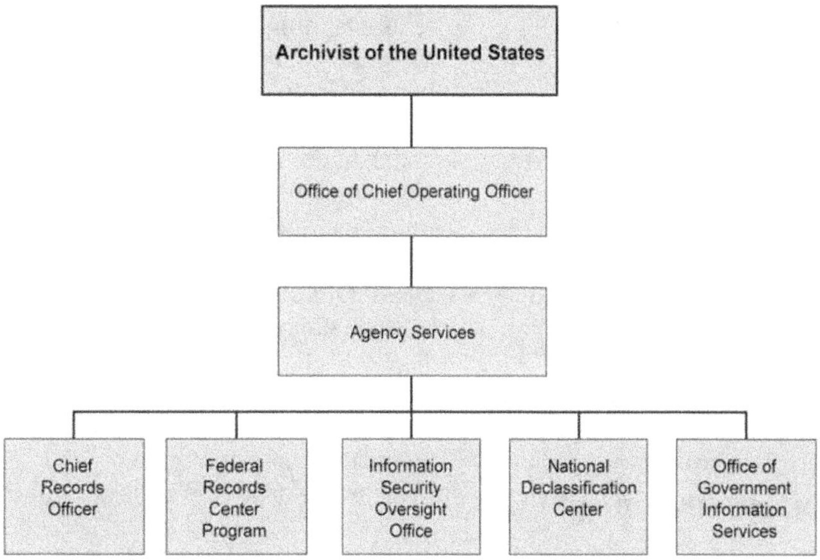

Source: National Archives and Records Administration.

Headquartered in Washington, D.C., OGIS is led by a director who reports to the Executive of Agency Services. As of August 2013, the Director was aided by a deputy director, an attorney advisor, two management and program analysts, and a staff assistant—for a total of six full-time employees.

Other Federal Agencies Also Have FOIA-Related Responsibilities	In addition to OGIS, other federal agencies also have responsibility for the oversight and administration of FOIA. Specifically, since it was established 30 years ago, the Office of Information Policy within the Department of Justice (Justice) has been responsible for overseeing the administration of FOIA by encouraging compliance, overseeing agencies' implementation of the *OPEN Government Act*, and issuing policy guidance. As such, the office prepares a comprehensive guide that addresses various aspects of the act; conducts a variety of FOIA-related training programs for personnel across the government; and uses attorneys to serve as counselors that provide FOIA information, advice, and guidance to government staff and the public regarding implementation of the act. In addition, Justice represents federal agencies in lawsuits brought by FOIA requesters.

According to Justice, as of fiscal year 2012, a total of 99 federal agencies had responsibility for implementing FOIA. These agencies process requests, publish related regulations, and submit annual reports through the heads of their agencies to the Attorney General that include statistics on their FOIA processing. Further, the *OPEN Government Act* gave agency chief FOIA officers responsibility for ensuring agencywide compliance by monitoring implementation throughout the agency; recommending changes in policies, practices, staffing, and funding; and reviewing and reporting to agency heads and to Justice on the agency's performance in implementing FOIA. (These reports are referred to as chief FOIA officer reports and are in addition to the annual reports that agencies also submit to Justice.) |
| **GAO Has Previously Reported on Agencies' Efforts to Implement FOIA** | Over the past 6 years, we have issued several reports on federal agencies' implementation of FOIA, including their progress in improving FOIA processing and backlog reduction.

- In 2007,[11] we reported on 25 major agencies' plans for improving FOIA processing and noted that most of the plans included goals and time tables addressing the areas of improvement emphasized by |

[11]GAO, *Freedom of Information Act: Processing Trends Show Importance of Improvement Plans*, GAO-07-441 (Washington, D.C.: Mar. 30, 2007) and *Freedom of Information Act: Processing Trends Show Importance of Improvement Plans*, GAO-07-491T (Washington, D.C.: Feb. 14, 2007).

Executive Order 13392,[12] which set forth a directive for a citizen-centered and results-oriented FOIA. In particular, the order directed agencies to provide requesters with courteous and appropriate service and ways to learn about the FOIA process, the status of their requests, and the public availability of other agency records. The order also instructed agencies to process requests efficiently, achieve measurable process improvements (including a reduction in the backlog of overdue requests), and reform programs that were not producing the appropriate results. However, certain agencies had omitted goals in areas where they were already considered to be strong. We noted that all the plans focused on making measurable improvements and formed a reasonable basis for carrying out the goals of the executive order, although the details in a few plans could be improved. Thus, among other things, we recommended that selected agencies strengthen their improvement plans. The agencies generally agreed with our recommendations and took actions to address them.

- In 2008,[13] we reported that, following the emphasis on backlog reduction in the executive order and agency improvement plans, many agencies had shown progress in decreasing their backlog of overdue requests. However, we identified several factors that contributed to the requests remaining open and recommended that, among other things, Justice provide additional guidance to agencies on tracking and reporting overdue requests and planning to meet future backlog goals. In response to our recommendation, Justice's Office of Information Policy developed guidance on tracking and reporting backlogged requests.

- More recently, in July 2012,[14] we reported that four agencies with large backlogs had taken actions to decrease their backlogs, reduce their use of exemptions, and make their FOIA records available to the public by electronic means. We noted, however, that not all agency components were ensuring that frequently requested records were being made available online. Also, we reported that agencies were not always taking advantage of best practices for FOIA processing by, for

---

[12]Executive Order 13392, *Improving Agency Disclosure of Information* (Washington, D.C.: Dec. 14, 2005).

[13]GAO, *Freedom of Information Act: Agencies Are Making Progress in Reducing Backlog, but Additional Guidance Is Needed*, GAO-08-344 (Washington, D.C.: Mar. 14, 2008).

[14]GAO, *Freedom of Information Act: Additional Actions Can Strengthen Agency Efforts to Improve Management*, GAO-12-828 (Washington, D.C.: July 2012).

example, using a single tracking system and providing requesters with the ability to track the status of their requests online. We recommended that the agencies improve the management of their FOIA programs by ensuring that actions were taken to reduce backlogs and the use of exemptions, improve FOIA libraries, and implement technology. Officials from the four agencies agreed or generally agreed with the recommendations.

OGIS Has Assisted Agencies, but Has Not Proactively Reviewed Agencies' FOIA Policies, Procedures, and Compliance

OGIS has engaged in several activities that, according to its officials, were intended to respond to the *OPEN Government Act* requirement that it review federal agencies' FOIA policies, procedures, and compliance. Specifically, OGIS has engaged in tasks such as making suggestions for improving the clarity and readability of agencies' proposed FOIA regulations and notices and offering general observations regarding agencies' correspondence. For example, in 2010 and 2011, the office reviewed the *Federal Register*[15] to identify when agencies had submitted FOIA regulations for public comment and then offered responses to the requests for comments on the proposed regulations. In this regard, OGIS offered comments on improving the contents of regulations that had been proposed by 18 agencies. Among the suggestions that it offered to one or more of these agencies were that they:

- provide requesters with an estimated amount of fees, including a breakdown of the fees for the time staff devote to searching, reviewing, and/or duplicating records for a FOIA request;
- add a statement to clarify the difference between a third-party request made under FOIA and a first-party request made under the *Privacy Act*;
- notify requesters in writing when their requests have been referred to another agency, and include the part of the request that has been referred and the name of the FOIA contact in that agency; and
- recognize the important statutory role of the FOIA Public Liaison in reducing delays, increasing transparency, and understanding the status of requests.

---

[15]Published by NARA, the *Federal Register* is the federal government's official daily publication for rules, proposed rules, and notices of federal agencies and organizations, as well as executive orders and other presidential documents.

In addition, as part of its actions taken to review policies and procedures, in 2011 and 2012 the office responded to agencies' requests in the *Federal Register* for public comments on *Privacy Act* system of records notices. The office commented on six such requests during these 2 years. For example, the office suggested that agencies include model language in their system of records notices that would allow OGIS to share information with the affected agency as a permitted disclosure under the *Privacy Act*. According to the officials, without the model language, OGIS would be required to obtain written consent from each requester prior to being able to access their records when mediating a dispute.

Further, through various means (for example, FOIA roundtable meetings, website, and blog) in 2012 and 2013, OGIS invited agencies to submit FOIA correspondence, such as acknowledgment and close-out letters, for its review. According to OGIS, one agency responded to these invitations and the office, in turn, made suggestions aimed at improving the clarity and readability of the agency's correspondence. Specifically, OGIS provided comments to the National Geospatial Intelligence Agency on a template for its close-out letter that clarified the legal requirements to protect from disclosure, information on the location of classified military systems personnel, and information on contractor proposals. Beyond this activity, the office offered Dispute Resolution Skills training to agencies, including the Departments of State, Homeland Security, and Health and Human Services, and, as part of the training, provided instruction on improving agency correspondence to requesters.

Nevertheless, while OGIS has engaged in these specific activities, none was a proactive, comprehensive evaluation of federal agencies' FOIA policies and procedures. Moreover, the office has not conducted any reviews of agencies' compliance with FOIA. Rather, the office has generally worked in an ad hoc, reactive manner to respond to Federal Register proposals put forth by agencies or to seek opportunities to comment or provide training on correspondence and documentation other than FOIA policies and procedures. Furthermore, the activities that it has undertaken have been limited to engaging with only a small fraction of the 99 federal agencies that, according to Justice, have responsibility for implementing FOIA. Similarly, while the office reported that it has reviewed agencies' annual FOIA reports and Chief FOIA Officer reports from Justice's Office of Information Policy website to identify best practices on improving FOIA processing, and has made general observations about agencies' policies, procedures, and compliance with FOIA through the office's mediation case work, these actions were not undertaken as part of a specific review of agencies' compliance with FOIA, as required by the *OPEN Government Act*.

A key factor contributing to the absence of proactive and comprehensive reviews of federal agencies' FOIA policies, procedures, and compliance by OGIS is that the office has not established a structured methodology for conducting such reviews. Our work has determined that developing a methodology is critical to conducting quality, credible, and useful reviews. Our evaluation guidance states that a structured methodology should define, among other things, the scope, schedule, criteria, and evaluation questions for conducting the reviews.[16] OGIS had not defined the scope of work for its reviews, to include information on which specific agencies it will review, (such as the agencies that receive the largest number of FOIA requests) and when it will do so. In addition, the office had not established the criteria against which the agencies' policies, procedures, and compliance with FOIA requirements would be assessed; and it had not developed evaluation questions to be used in conducting the reviews.

The Director of OGIS acknowledged the limitations of the reviews that had been conducted, stating that the office had prioritized its resources to favor mediation activities. In this regard, the Director stated that the staff tasked with providing mediation services should function as neutral third parties and be independent from staff tasked with reviewing agencies' FOIA policies, procedures, and compliance. However, the Director said that, given the small number of staff assigned to OGIS, the office has not been able to establish a separate team of reviewers. OGIS officials added that the office is in the early stages of drafting a methodology for conducting the reviews, but that a time frame for when the methodology will be completed has not been established. Further, while Agency Services has identified a need for additional staff to support OGIS in implementing its mission, it has not established a plan that addresses how the office intends to staff the FOIA reviews. Industry practices stress the importance of analyzing workforce needs and developing a plan of action for addressing those needs. Moreover, in September 2012, a report issued by the Office of Inspector General at NARA concluded that while OGIS was currently able to meet its mission, additional resources would allow the office to have a more robust program for conducting the

---

[16]GAO, *Designing Evaluations: 2012 Revision*, GAO-12-208G (Washington, D.C.: January 2012).

reviews.[17] The Office of Inspector General recommended that the Director of OGIS, through the budget process, define resources necessary to better accomplish the office's statutory requirement. As of early August 2013, however, OGIS had not yet implemented this recommendation.

Until OGIS completes a methodology, and defines the resources needed to accomplish the requirements of the office as the NARA Inspector General has recommended, the office will not be positioned to effectively execute the responsibilities envisioned for it in assisting with this important aspect of FOIA implementation.

OGIS Is Mediating Disputes, but Lacks Goals and Metrics for Measuring Timeliness and Success

In response to the OPEN Government Act requirement that it offer mediation services to resolve disputes between FOIA requesters and agencies as a non-exclusive alternative to litigation, OGIS defines two types of mediation services that it provides to address requests for assistance:[18]

- **Facilitation**: A type of mediation in which an OGIS staff member facilitates communication between the requester and the agency, helping the parties to reach a mutually agreeable solution without the perceived formality or cost of mediation.
- **Ombuds services**: Advice and services (other than mediation) offered in response to complaints that the office receives. Ombuds services do not address the substance of a dispute (such as the exemptions taken), but rather, the mechanics of a dispute (such as the status of a delayed request).

OGIS has a documented process for handling the requests that it receives. Specifically, when a request is received—by phone, e-mail, fax, or electronically through its website—a case file is opened and assigned a tracking number in an automated case management system. Once a case has been opened, the office goes through a fact-finding process to determine what services are called for, such as, helping the parties exchange information or suggesting options for resolution. For each case,

[17]Office of Inspector General, National Archives and Records Administration, *Audit of NARA's Office of Government Information Services* (September 2012).

[18]OGIS also handles what it calls "quick hits"—requests for assistance that can be answered immediately—such as how to file a FOIA request or an appeal.

further actions taken by OGIS and the other parties involved, as well as any agreements reached, are recorded in the case management system.

During fiscal year 2012, OGIS accepted 855 requests for assistance: 46 involved facilitation or both facilitation/ombuds services, and 239 involved only ombuds services. Of the remaining requests, 498 were classified by OGIS as a "quick hit"[19] and 72 were classified as miscellaneous (for example, "administrative closure," "no direct action requested," or "request withdrawn.")

Of the 44 facilitation and facilitation/ombuds services cases that OGIS initiated in 2012,[20] the office provided mediation for 30. (Most of the remaining 14 were cases that OGIS did not mediate because it agreed with the agency's decision on the FOIA request.) Further, among the cases that were mediated, we determined that 22 had a positive result, as defined by one or more of the following three actions:

- **One or both parties took action or modified their position after OGIS's intervention.** For example, a requester conducting family genealogy research requested from the Social Security Administration, a copy of a Social Security form pertaining to a family member. In response, the agency sent the form to the requester, but the subject's parents' names had been redacted—blacked out—because the Social Security Administration does not reveal information about a living person and, given their dates of birth, had concluded that the parents might still be alive. The requester filed an appeal and provided death certificates for the parents, but the appeal was denied. An OGIS mediator subsequently contacted a Social Security Administration official on the requester's behalf to discuss the denial. After reexamining the case, the agency agreed to send an unredacted document to the requester.

---

[19]A quick hit is not considered to be a case, but is entered into the case management system. It does not involve mediation services but is a request for assistance that can be answered immediately, such as a question about how to file a FOIA request or whom to contact at an agency to get information about a request.

[20]While 46 cases were initiated in 2012, we included 44 cases in our review. One case was omitted because it involved only OGIS and agency officials, and a second was omitted because the case was not included in the data OGIS provided from which we made our selection.

- **One or both parties indicated increased satisfaction with the outcome of the FOIA process as a result of OGIS's mediation.** For example, a representative of a trade organization, who had requested contract data from the Department of Homeland Security, had received only part of the information requested. The agency withheld substantial information under a FOIA exemption protecting trade secrets. The requester subsequently contacted OGIS, and a mediator contacted the agency's appeals officer and discussed the relevant case law. In response to this action, the agency reconsidered its decision and provided the information with only minimal redactions. The customer noted that she was "extremely happy with the results of the mediation."
- **The issue in dispute was clarified, addressed, or resolved after OGIS intervened.** For example, a requester asked the Securities and Exchange Commission for all its files of a certain type and later asked OGIS for help because of a perceived delay in the agency's response. A mediator then contacted an official at the agency, who explained that the requested files were difficult to retrieve because some were paper files that were not indexed and were geographically dispersed. The mediator explained this to the requester, who was initially unwilling to compromise but was open to an OGIS-facilitated discussion with the agency. The agency agreed, and OGIS subsequently facilitated a teleconference between the requester and the agency, during which the two parties agreed that the requester would file a narrower request that the agency could fill promptly.

Overall, among these 22 cases, 9 involved a *denial*, in which an agency declined to release the requested records; 7 involved a delay, in which a requester believed the agency was taking too much time to fill a request; and 3 involved *fees*, where a requester believed the amount being charged was excessive or that a fee waiver was applicable.[21] The other 3 cases involved: a dispute over whether an appeal had been submitted in a timely manner, a customer disputing that an agency had not found responsive records, and a requester wanting results in a different format.

---

[21]Agencies may charge fees for search and copying, but there are exceptions. For example, news media pay reduced or no fees. For all requesters, fees may be waived if disclosure of the information is in the public interest because it is likely to contribute significantly to public understanding of the operations or activities of the government and is not primarily in the commercial interest of the requester.

GAO-13-650 OGIS's FOIA Responsibilities

Also, among the cases that OGIS mediated, we determined that 8 did not have a positive result, as explained by the following examples:

- In four cases, OGIS provided mediation services, but the agency did not change its position on refusing to provide the requested information. In one case, for example, the agency did not change its position that the requester needed to provide a waiver or proof of death for the subject of the request in order for the agency to process the request. In another example, the agency stood by its decision to refer the requester to a publicly available document.
- In one case, the agency, after its initial meeting with OGIS and the requester, was unwilling to continue to meet on matters related to the FOIA request.
- In one case, OGIS held discussions regarding the agency not granting the requester free search time as required by FOIA and OMB's guidance. The agency did not change its position and the requester pursued litigation regarding the matter.
- In the remaining two cases, OGIS confirmed that the information the requesters were seeking was either exempt from disclosure, or the record did not exist. For example, in one of these cases, the requester had sought a list of active Internal Revenue Service tax-exempt cases in litigation, but had received a "no records" response from the agency. As part of its mediation efforts, OGIS confirmed that the agency did not keep the requested information in any of its records.

Of the 14 cases where mediation was not provided, 11 were cases where OGIS agreed with the agency's decision to deny a request. For example, in one of the cases, a prison inmate requested a copy of the Bureau of Prisons *Correctional Services Manual*, which addresses the operations of federal prisons. The bureau withheld the manual under a law enforcement exemption, stating that, while there may have been a public interest in the material, that interest did not outweigh the need to keep order in the prison system and avoid inmates using the information to their advantage. The requester then contacted OGIS, and the office responded that the agency's actions had been consistent with FOIA law and policy and declined to mediate. In another instance, a case was not mediated because the agency declined to cooperate with OGIS. Further, for the remaining 2 cases, OGIS ultimately determined that they were ones in which mediation was not needed. For example, to resolve one of the cases, OGIS only needed to explain an agency letter to a requester.

Although it has taken actions to resolve disputes—in many cases having positive results through mediation—the office lacks performance measures and goals needed to gauge the overall success of its mediation services. *The Government Performance and Results Act Modernization Act of 2010*[22] requires NARA, like all agencies, to develop an annual performance plan that includes performance goals for its program activities and accompanying performance measures, including timeliness and results-based measures. According to the act, the performance goals should be in a quantifiable and measurable form to define the level of performance to be achieved for program activities each year. Measuring performance allows an agency to track the progress it is making toward goals and gives managers crucial information on which to base their organizational and management decisions. Leading organizations recognize that performance measures can create powerful incentives to influence organizational and individual behavior.

However, consistent with its fiscal year 2013 annual report, in which the office states that it has no formal metrics for measuring success, OGIS has not developed measures and goals for its mediation services. While its case management system can track the length of time required to handle a particular case, the office currently has no specific goals related to timeliness in handling requests for assistance. In this regard, in fiscal year 2012, the office had a timeliness goal, derived from NARA's overall performance plan, of closing cases within 34 working days. However, according to the officials, this goal was dropped because it was not based on the office's actual experience in handling the cases.[23]

OGIS also has no measures or goals pertaining to the results of its mediation cases. For example, it has not established criteria for determining what constitutes success in a case or a goal for what percentage of its cases should have a successful result. OGIS's Director said that the office is aware of the need for such measures and is making efforts to meet the need. The Director told us that OGIS has engaged a consultant to help review its case management system, identify reasons for differing case closure times, and help develop more measurable milestones. However, OGIS had not implemented measures as of mid-August 2013. Further, the office has begun using an online questionnaire where its customers can provide anonymous feedback on their

[22]Pub. L. No. 111-352, (Jan. 4, 2011), 124 Stat. 3866.

[23]In fact, OGIS reports that its cases were open an average of 89.5 days in fiscal year 2012.

experiences with OGIS and its staff. While this questionnaire may be useful if enough responses are received,[24] its value as a voluntary, Web-based survey is limited: its respondents are self-selected, responses are anonymous, and comments cannot be linked to specific cases or contexts, thus limiting their usefulness. Until OGIS establishes quantifiable goals and measures of success for its mediation services, the office will not be positioned to determine how effectively it is performing mediation and contributing to the resolution of cases that might otherwise have resulted in potentially costly litigation or gone unresolved.

OGIS Has Made Recommendations and Issued Best Practices for Improving the Administration of FOIA

As required by the *OPEN Government Act,* OGIS has made recommendations to Congress and the President aimed at improving the administration of FOIA. These recommendations have largely focused on improving the internal coordination of government FOIA operations and areas where OGIS's role could be made more effective. In addition, while it has not issued specific guidance on FOIA implementation, OGIS has collected best practices for improving FOIA processing for federal agencies.

Altogether, OGIS has made nine recommendations aimed at improving the FOIA process—five in 2012 and four in 2013. Seven of the recommendations were specific to actions that the office believed it should take (in certain cases in conjunction with agency partners and other stakeholders), while two of the recommendations focused on actions to be taken by other federal agencies.

Specifically, OGIS recommended to Congress and the President actions that it had either taken or was planning to take to enhance its own role in administering FOIA, as follows:

- Work to encourage other departments and agencies to partner with it to expand dispute resolution training for their FOIA professionals so that they can assist their FOIA colleagues in preventing and resolving disputes.

---

[24]OGIS had received only one response in the first 5 months the survey was available.

- Work with other agencies to consider how the FOIA web portal (https://FOIAonline.regulations.gov/),[25] the governmentwide FOIA portal, might be useful to them in carrying out their statutory responsibilities and use it to accept FOIA requests and allow responsive documents to be uploaded and posted for the public.
- Facilitate the coordination of interagency communication for governmentwide FOIA requests among agencies by serving as the central point-of-contact for agencies in sharing information, and also for relaying information to requesters as appropriate.
- Work with stakeholders from both inside and outside government to review the issues surrounding FOIA fees and fee waivers, which remains a persistent point of contention administratively and in litigation.
- Develop, with the Chief Information Officers Council, methods for agencies to better handle requesters seeking their own records under the *Privacy Act* to improve how requesters navigate agency processes to obtain needed assistance.
- In conjunction with OMB, create a governmentwide Privacy Act routine-use procedure to streamline the way in which agencies share with OGIS information covered by the act.
- Work with agencies to streamline the process of requesting immigration-related records because of the increased number of requests related to these records.

In addition, OGIS recommended that federal agencies take specific actions, as follows:

- Encourage and support the use of dispute resolution in the agency FOIA processes to prevent and resolve disputes administratively and avoid litigation.
- Remind their staff of the importance of FOIA and recognize FOIA as a priority (based on the position that many agency employees may be unfamiliar with their own responsibilities under the law).

OGIS officials stated that the recommendations were based on the office's ongoing work with federal agencies and members of the public. They acknowledged that the office had not compiled other information

---

[25]The website offers requesters one place to submit FOIA requests, track their progress, communicate with the processing agency, search other requests, access previously released responsive documents, and file appeals with participating agencies.

that would be necessary to recommend substantive revisions to underlying FOIA policies or otherwise suggest legislative actions to Congress and the President. However, such information potentially could have been derived if OGIS had taken steps to conduct more comprehensive reviews of agencies' FOIA policies, procedures, and compliance and had established and implemented results-based measures for its mediation services.

According to its documentation, OGIS submitted the nine recommendations over a 2-year period from February 2011 through March 2013. The officials explained that their submission of these recommendations followed periods of interagency review as required under the process overseen by OMB. Specifically, they explained that OGIS had submitted its first two draft recommendations for review in accordance with the OMB Circular A-19[26] on February 16, 2011. These initial recommendations focused on developing, with the Chief Information Officers Council, methods for agencies to better handle requesters seeking their own records under the *Privacy Act* and in conjunction with OMB, creating a governmentwide *Privacy Act* routine-use procedure. Then, over the next 14 months, OMB and NARA had periodic discussions regarding the significant number of interagency comments that OMB had received on the recommendations.

Following discussion on the status of the two recommendations at a congressional hearing in March 2012,[27] OGIS submitted three additional recommendations to OMB for review. OMB officials said they then worked with OGIS to address interagency comments on the three recommendations, as well as the initial two recommendations.

---

[26]OMB Circular A-19, *Legislative Coordination and Clearance* (Sept. 20, 1979), requires federal agencies to submit to OMB for review proposed legislation, testimonies, reports, and other documents they intend to submit to Congress. According to the circular, OMB performs legislative coordination and clearance functions to (a) assist the President in developing a position on legislation, (b) make known the administration's position on legislation for the guidance of the agencies and information of Congress, (c) assure appropriate consideration of the views of all affected agencies, and (d) assist the President with respect to action on enrolled bills. According to OMB, the length of this review varies depending on the comments provided by the agencies.

[27]The hearing, entitled "The Freedom of Information Act: Safeguarding Critical Infrastructure Information and the Public's Right to Know," was held on March13, 2012, by the Senate Judiciary Committee.

After OMB completed its review in mid-April 2012, OGIS informed Congress[28] that its recommendations did not include any substantive revisions to the disclosure requirements of FOIA. OGIS officials subsequently stated that, as a result of the interagency consultation process, OGIS and OMB had agreed that the five recommendations could be addressed administratively and did not require any legislative action.

In mid-January 2013, OGIS and OMB officials met to discuss a second set of potential recommendations that the office intended to submit. The office subsequently submitted four recommendations to OMB for Circular A-19 review on March 4, 2013. According to OGIS officials, the review of these recommendations was completed on March 12, 2013, and the recommendations were provided to Congress on March 13, 2013, to support a congressional hearing during Sunshine Week.[29]

OGIS Does Not Issue Guidance, but Disseminates Best Practices for Improving FOIA Processing

Although OGIS does not issue specific guidance on FOIA implementation,[30] it collects and shares best practices for improving federal agencies' processing of FOIA requests. According to OMB, best practices are the processes, practices, and systems identified in public and private organizations that work exceptionally well and are widely recognized as being helpful in improving an organization's performance and efficiency in specific areas. Best practices can be based on lessons learned from positive experiences or on negative experiences that result in an undesirable outcome. In addition, guidance states that the use of

[28]Letter from the Director of OGIS to Chairman Patrick Leahy and Ranking Member Charles Grassley, Senate Judiciary Committee, Apr. 13, 2012.

[29]Sunshine Week is a national initiative to promote a dialogue about the importance of open government and freedom of information. Participants include news media, civic groups, libraries, nonprofits, schools, and others interested in the public's right to access to information.

[30]The OPEN Government Act does not require OGIS to issue guidance. Justice's Office of Information Policy is responsible for developing, coordinating, and implementing policy and guidance under a regulation authorizing it to exercise the functions vested in the Attorney General by FOIA. 28 C.F.R.0.24.

best practices is a principal component of an organizational culture committed to continuous improvement.[31]

Toward this end, OGIS collects best practices for improving FOIA processing from several sources, including its reviews of agencies' annual FOIA reports and mediation case files, as well as anecdotally from persons involved in mediation cases facilitated by the office. OGIS publishes best practices related to key FOIA requirements and guidance in its annual reports, and on its website (https://ogis.archives.gov/) and blog (http://blogs.archives.gov/foiablog/). The website includes a number of links describing various best practices specifically for FOIA requestors and federal agencies. Table 1 describes examples of the best practices OGIS has disseminated.

Table 1: Examples of OGIS Best Practices for Improving Agencies' Implementation of FOIA

Selected best practice	Description
Communications and customer service	Agencies should post in plain language information about fees, fee categories, and fee waivers.
	Once a FOIA request has been received and acknowledged, an agency can continue to practice good customer service communication. For example, one approach is to create an online system to allow a requester to easily check the status of their request.
	Agencies should provide in writing to the requester the tracking number and contact information for the FOIA Public Liaison and the FOIA professional assigned to the case as quickly as possible.
FOIA database requests	Involve the requester early on, particularly if the requester is a database expert. Many are willing to share their knowledge with agencies to help move the FOIA process forward. Take them up on any offers to share their expertise and consider allowing them to talk directly with the IT staff to discuss the best approaches for responding to their request.
Agency FOIA regulations	For drafting FOIA regulations, agencies should bring attorneys, FOIA processors, records managers, and IT professionals to the table. Each will bring a different perspective—plus, a well-organized team can lighten the load for a single person on a tedious but important task.
Contacting requesters	Contact with requesters need not always be by mail. Often, it may be more efficient to contact the requester by e-mail or by telephone; these messages can be memorialized in writing later.
Tracking requests	Provide in writing to the requester the tracking number and contact information for the FOIA Public Liaison as quickly as possible.

Source: GAO analysis of OGIS best practices.

---

[31]Aha, D., Becerra-Fernandez, I., and Weber, R., *Categorizing Intelligent Lessons Learned Systems*, Technical Report AIC-00-005. (Washington, D.C.: Naval Research Laboratory, Navy Center for Applied Research in Artificial Intelligence. 2000), 63-67.

OGIS officials stated that the office updates its blog at least weekly with posts addressing best practices, case studies, and where the public and federal agencies can engage in discussions about FOIA issues. In addition, OGIS uses other mechanisms to improve the administration of FOIA, to include presenting training for FOIA professionals; holding conferences with the American Society for Access Professionals to share best practices; and, at the start of fiscal year 2013, helping to launch the FOIA web portal (https://FOIAonline.regulations.gov/).

Conclusions

Since it was established 4 years ago, OGIS has taken actions to implement selected legislative responsibilities, although it has fallen short in certain areas. Specifically, while the office has suggested improvements to a number of agencies' FOIA regulations and system of records notices, it has not completed a methodology for proactively reviewing agencies' policies, procedures, and compliance with FOIA requirements and a time frame for doing so. As a mediator between requesters and federal agencies, OGIS has resolved cases that might have otherwise resulted in litigation. However, while we were able to identify instances in which its mediation efforts have had positive results, the office's overall success in mediating cases is difficult to gauge without goals and performance measures. On the basis of its reviews of agency policy and procedures, and mediation experience, OGIS has made a number of recommendations to Congress and the President and shared best practices to help agencies improve the administration of FOIA. However, addressing the shortfalls that we noted is critical to OGIS effectively complying with its role as required by law.

Recommendations

To ensure that OGIS effectively performs its responsibilities under FOIA, as amended by the *OPEN Government Act,* we recommend that the Archivist of the United States direct the Executive for Agency Services and the Director of OGIS to take the following two actions:

- Establish a time frame for completing and implementing a methodology that defines, among other things, the scope, schedule, criteria, and evaluation questions for conducting reviews of federal agencies' FOIA policies, procedures, and compliance.

- Establish performance measures and goals for OGIS's mediation services that define success in handling a case and include relevant goals for the number of cases handled successfully, as well as goals for timely management of cases based on past experience.

Agency Comments and Our Evaluation

We provided drafts of this report to NARA and OMB for comment. In its written comments, which are reprinted in appendix II, NARA expressed appreciation for our attention to issues facing OGIS and concurred with the two recommendations in the report. NARA also specifically discussed actions that it was taking or planned to take related to our second recommendation. In particular, the agency stated that OGIS has consulted with other mediation and ombudsman offices on how to evaluate its services and will continue to do so. NARA added that it has been difficult to measure success and that the office's resolution of a dispute is dependent on outside factors that are beyond OGIS's control, such as the willingness of the parties to participate in voluntary mediation services. Further, NARA stated that it appreciated our suggestions regarding measures for success and would consider these suggestions as the office assesses measures for the upcoming fiscal year.

In addition to the aforementioned written comments, we received technical comments, via e-mail, from NARA's Audit Liaison and OMB's Audit Liaison, which we have incorporated, as appropriate.

We are sending copies of this report to the appropriate congressional committees; the Archivist of the United States; Executive for Agency Services, Director of OGIS, and other interested parties. Copies of this report will also be available at no charge on the GAO Web site, at http://www.gao.gov.

Should you or your staffs have any questions on the information discussed in this report, please contact me at (202) 512-6304 or melvinv@gao.gov. Contact points for our Offices of Congressional Relations and Public Affairs may be found on the last page of this report. GAO staff who made major contributions to this report are listed in appendix III.

Valerie C. Melvin
Director, Information Management
and Technology Resources Issues

Appendix I: Objectives, Scope, and Methodology

Our objectives were to assess the actions that the Office of Government Information Services (OGIS) has taken to (1) review agencies' *Freedom of Information Act* (FOIA) policies, procedures, and compliance, (2) mediate disputes between FOIA requesters and federal agencies, and (3) recommend policy changes to Congress and the President, and develop and issue guidance and best practices to agencies aimed at improving the administration of FOIA.

To assess the actions OGIS has taken to review agencies' FOIA policies, procedures, and compliance, we analyzed documentation describing the office's plans and activities for conducting agency FOIA reviews. These included the office's annual reports for fiscal years 2011 through 2013, quarterly reports, NARA's annual performance plan for fiscal years 2011 through 2013, and the office's comments on 18 proposed agency regulations and six Privacy Act system of records notices. We analyzed OGIS's comments on agency FOIA correspondence, such as closeout letters, and training materials on improving agency correspondence to requesters. We compared the plans and activities to our program evaluation guidance[1] that focuses on assessing the effectiveness of program operations and results. We also analyzed OGIS's comments on the proposed agency regulations and compared them to the latest version of the agency's regulations to determine whether they were incorporated.

To assess the actions that OGIS has taken to mediate disputes between requesters and federal agencies, we reviewed the *Administrative Dispute Resolution Act of 1996*; published literature on mediation and alternative dispute resolution; and our prior work on alternative dispute resolution. We discussed the office's activities with its officials, reviewed its mediation process and definitions, and compared them with third-party sources. We attended training on dispute resolution that was presented by OGIS. We also reviewed the initial results of the office's online customer survey. We then selected the 44 cases[2] that had been initiated in 2012 and that were characterized by OGIS as involving facilitation. We

---

[1]GAO, *Designing Evaluations: 2012 Revision*, GAO-12-208G (Washington, D.C.: January 2012) and *Program Evaluation: Studies Helped Agencies Measure or Explain Program Performance*, GAO/GGD-00-204 (Washington, D.C.: Sept. 29, 2000).

[2]While 46 cases were initiated in 2012, we included 44 cases in our review. We omitted two cases: one because it involved only OGIS and the agency's FOIA staff, and one because it was not included in the data that OGIS provided, and from which we made our selection.

examined the corresponding paper case files as well as data from the
office's automated case tracking system.

We developed criteria, after discussions with OGIS, for verifying whether
a case involved mediation and for determining the result of the office's
mediation efforts. Specifically, we verified that a case was an example of
mediation if one of the following occurred:

- Other than the initial contact, OGIS had two or more substantive
  contacts with either party.
- The office suggested options for changing a position or decision to
  either party.
- Either party changed a decision or position (e.g. the agency waived
  fees or provided additional documents, or the requester narrowed the
  scope of a request).

We considered the office's mediation efforts to have had a positive result
if at least one of the following events occurred:

- One or both parties took some action or modified their position after
  OGIS's intervention (for example, the agency reduced fees or
  provided further documents).
- One or both parties indicated increased satisfaction with the outcome
  of the FOIA process as the result of the office's mediation.
- The issue in dispute was clarified, addressed, or resolved.

To determine the reliability of data from OGIS's case tracking system, we
performed basic steps to ensure the data provided were valid and
reviewed relevant information describing the database. Specifically, we
tested for duplicate records, missing values, and out-of-range values in
the data received from OGIS. We assessed the reliability of the system
used to maintain these data. To determine the reliability of the case data,
we independently replicated a report generated by the software and
compared it to documents provided by OGIS to determine whether the
data matched. Also, we conducted interviews with agency officials to gain
an understanding of the process by which data are entered and validated.
Based on the results of these efforts, we found the data sources to be
sufficiently reliable for our purposes.

To assess the office's actions to recommend policy changes to Congress
and the President, we reviewed documentation describing policy
recommendations that were made to Congress and the President. We
analyzed annual reports on the status of the implementation of these

recommendations. In addition, we reviewed the Office of Management
and Budget's (OMB) written responses describing its reviews of OGIS's
policy recommendations, as well as any applicable OMB guidance, such
as the Circular A-19. We supplemented our analyses with interviews of
the Director of OGIS, the Acting Executive for Agency Services (the
NARA organization in which OGIS is located), officials from OMB's Office
of General Counsel, and other cognizant NARA and OGIS officials. To
assess OGIS's actions to provide best practices to federal agencies, we
reviewed documentation of OGIS's agency best practices, case studies,
and suggestions regarding FOIA included in the annual reports, and on
the website and blog. We also observed OGIS meetings with other
agencies, FOIA requesters, and the general public to discuss FOIA
topics, such as the administration of fees and access to records through
FOIA libraries. We supplemented our analyses with interviews of relevant
OGIS officials to discuss the process used to identify best practices and
measures established to evaluate their use by federal agencies.

We conducted this performance audit from October 2012 through
September 2013 in accordance with generally accepted government
auditing standards. Those standards require that we plan and perform the
audit to obtain sufficient, appropriate evidence to provide a reasonable
basis for our findings and conclusions based on our audit objectives. We
believe that the evidence obtained provides a reasonable basis for our
findings and conclusions based on our audit objectives.

Appendix II: Comments from the National Archives and Records Administration

NATIONAL
ARCHIVES

ARCHIVIST *of the*
UNITED STATES

DAVID S. FERRIERO
T: 202.357.5900
F: 202.357.5901
david.ferriero@nara.gov

27 August 2013

Valerie C. Melvin
Director, Information Management and Technology Team
United States Government Accountability Office
44 G Street, NW
Washington, DC 20548

Dear Ms. Melvin:

Thank you for the opportunity to review and comment on the Government Accountability Office's (GAO's) draft report 13-650 titled "Office of Government Information Services Has Begun Implementing Its Responsibilities, but Further Actions are Needed." We appreciate your attention to issues facing our Office of Government Information Services (OGIS). The report contains two recommendations for Executive Action. NARA concurs with both recommendations.

The challenge of how to evaluate the success of mediation services is not unique to OGIS. Other government ombudsman offices struggle with the same issue. OGIS has consulted with other mediation and ombudsman offices on how to evaluate its services and it will continue to do so. In mediating FOIA disputes, it is difficult to measure success in terms of an outcome. Moreover, OGIS's resolution of a dispute is dependent on outside factors beyond OGIS's control, such as the willingness of the parties to participate in voluntary mediation services.

OGIS has identified performance goals and targets for each year since its creation, which are reported in NARA's Performance & Accountability Report. NARA annually assesses measurement of its programs and develops new measurements as business needs dictate. We appreciate the auditor's suggestions regarding measures for success. We will consider these suggestions as we assess measures for the upcoming fiscal year.

If you have any questions regarding this memo please contact Jay Trainer, Executive for Agency Services, at 301-837-0634 or via email at jay.trainer@nara.gov.

Sincerely,

DAVID S. FERRIERO
Archivist of the United States

Via email to: Valerie C. Melvin, MelvinV@gao.gov; Cynthia Scott, ScottC@gao.gov; Freda Paintsil, PaintsilF@gao.gov

NATIONAL ARCHIVES *and*
RECORDS ADMINISTRATION
700 PENNSYLVANIA AVENUE, NW
WASHINGTON, DC 20408-0001
www.archives.gov

Appendix III: GAO Contact and Staff Acknowledgments

GAO Contact	Valerie C. Melvin, (202) 512-6304 or melvinv@gao.gov
Staff Acknowledgments	In addition to the contact named above, key contributors to this report were Cynthia J. Scott (assistant director), Nancy Glover, Cynthia Grant, Ashfaq Huda, Alina J. Johnson, Ruben Montes de Oca, Freda Paintsil, David Plocher, Glenn Spiegel, and Walter Vance.

GAO's Mission	The Government Accountability Office, the audit, evaluation, and investigative arm of Congress, exists to support Congress in meeting its constitutional responsibilities and to help improve the performance and accountability of the federal government for the American people. GAO examines the use of public funds; evaluates federal programs and policies; and provides analyses, recommendations, and other assistance to help Congress make informed oversight, policy, and funding decisions. GAO's commitment to good government is reflected in its core values of accountability, integrity, and reliability.
Obtaining Copies of GAO Reports and Testimony	The fastest and easiest way to obtain copies of GAO documents at no cost is through GAO's website (http://www.gao.gov). Each weekday afternoon, GAO posts on its website newly released reports, testimony, and correspondence. To have GAO e-mail you a list of newly posted products, go to http://www.gao.gov and select "E-mail Updates."
Order by Phone	The price of each GAO publication reflects GAO's actual cost of production and distribution and depends on the number of pages in the publication and whether the publication is printed in color or black and white. Pricing and ordering information is posted on GAO's website, http://www.gao.gov/ordering.htm. Place orders by calling (202) 512-6000, toll free (866) 801-7077, or TDD (202) 512-2537. Orders may be paid for using American Express, Discover Card, MasterCard, Visa, check, or money order. Call for additional information.
Connect with GAO	Connect with GAO on Facebook, Flickr, Twitter, and YouTube. Subscribe to our RSS Feeds or E-mail Updates. Listen to our Podcasts. Visit GAO on the web at www.gao.gov.
To Report Fraud, Waste, and Abuse in Federal Programs	Contact: Website: http://www.gao.gov/fraudnet/fraudnet.htm E-mail: fraudnet@gao.gov Automated answering system: (800) 424-5454 or (202) 512-7470
Congressional Relations	Katherine Siggerud, Managing Director, siggerudk@gao.gov, (202) 512-4400, U.S. Government Accountability Office, 441 G Street NW, Room 7125, Washington, DC 20548
Public Affairs	Chuck Young, Managing Director, youngc1@gao.gov, (202) 512-4800 U.S. Government Accountability Office, 441 G Street NW, Room 7149 Washington, DC 20548

www.ingramcontent.com/pod-product-compliance
Lightning Source LLC
Chambersburg PA
CBHW080744290526
45790CB00008B/3323